Someone to
Believe In

Someone to Believe In

Believe In

An Advent Course based on
Miracle on 34th Street

SHEILA JACOBS

DARTON·LONGMAN + TODD

First published in 2015 by
Darton, Longman and Todd Ltd
1 Spencer Court
140 – 142 Wandsworth High Street
London SW18 4JJ

ISBN 978-0-232-53190-9

All Scripture quotations are taken from the New International Version
(NIV, 2011) unless otherwise stated.

A catalogue record for this book is available from the British Library

Designed and produced by Judy Linard

Printed and bound by Imak Ofset, Turkey

Contents

Introduction   7

WEEK ONE   15
Seeds of Faith

WEEK TWO   37
Friends and Enemies

WEEK THREE   65
When Common Sense
Tells You Not To

WEEK FOUR   83
Nothing Impossible

Conclusion   107

Introduction

Christmas! The familiar songs, the tree, the decorations, the turkey, the old tea towels on the heads of small shepherds singing 'Away in a Manger', the frantic buying of food even though the shops are only shut for two days .... Some of my neighbours have their decorations up by 1 December! In fact, I have noticed one or two houses in the small town where I live don't bother to take plastic Santa off the roof at all. He is parked there all year round.

Ask people about Christmas, and you get a variety of answers, of course. 'Oooh, I love Christmas with all the family!' And then there is the more dismissive, 'It's a time for children. But I like the parties.' Or, at the other end of the scale, 'Christmas? It's too commercialized. It's all about money.' Or, 'Best thing about Christmas is the Boxing Day sales.'

We also have to be aware that Christmas can be an intensely difficult time for those who are alone, or for those who find the hyped-up view of family life painful in the light of their own less-than-perfect experiences.

For me, I remember happy Christmases of childhood with all the glue and glitter and Nativity plays, presents under the tree and smiling grandparents. However, I also seem to have a picture in my mind of ice-skating (I've never done it) and cottages and old churches covered in snow (I don't remember heavy snow at Christmas, ever, and we didn't live in the country when I was a child). I suspect my memories stem from romantic Christmas cards.

And that's the problem. Christmas is all mixed up.

In all the rush and panic of December – and even before that – when it comes to Christmas, we forget what the season is meant to be about. Although some people accurately point out that Jesus wasn't born in December – more likely in the autumn – and that we are actually taking part in an ancient pagan festival, for believers and those who would like to know more, the central figure of the season is and should be Jesus. It is quite true that the early Christian Church 'Christianized' Saturnalia, a Roman festival, but it's good to celebrate God's gift of Jesus to the world; and why not do it in mid-winter?

However, the old pagan festival still remains. The awesome truth about the God-man coming to earth to pay the price we could never pay so we could get right with God is mixed in with 'Rudolph, the Red-Nosed Reindeer'. Last Christmas, I attended a 'carol service' of sorts, children singing for elderly folk, where the songs were a mixture of 'Once in Royal David's City', 'Away in a Manger' and 'Frosty the Snowman'. This is Christmas as magical fantasy, where the real supernatural element is watered down, counted the same as Frosty and Rudolph, and ultimately becomes unbelievable. Children are encouraged to believe in a benevolent Father Christmas, who then turns out to be fictional, although his roots lie in history; and cute baby Jesus, just a part of the celebrations, stays safely in a manger. Let's face it, if as a child you discover that Santa's just a magical figure and not real, then why should Jesus be any different?

In this little book, we are going to use Santa Claus for our own purposes. If that sounds a bit sinister, don't worry. We're going to look at the film *Miracle on 34th Street*, which is a sweet story about faith, about believing in a man who is claiming to be someone that sensible grown-ups don't believe in. Here, we'll think about issues of faith in relation to the person we are really celebrating at Christmas – Jesus. We'll think about who he claimed to be, and how those claims affect us today.

Now, it's difficult to find time during this hectic season to get alone with God, let alone think about an Advent study, but it's good to focus the mind on the big questions that often get lost in the Christmas tears and tantrums (and that's just the adults). I should also mention that this book doesn't strictly follow the four weekly Advent themes you may be used to, if you are a member of a more traditional denomination: that is, hope, peace, joy and love. But you will find these interwoven with the main theme of faith.

You may like to read this book with a home group, with a few friends, or alone. I have made sure to include reflections and activities that can be carried out on your own as well as in a small group. I have used the plural in prayers, for convenience, although you might change the 'we' to 'I' if you prefer. The study is interactive; as well as clips from the film, there are activities, reflection, discussion and prayers at the end of the weeks. Also, there are 'pause for thought' questions that might lead to discussions and deeper thinking if you have the time. It may be that you choose to read a 'week' over seven days, breaking it up as you find space to seek Jesus over the Advent period.

Before you begin to read, I suggest you watch the film. The studies are based on the original (1947) version, starring Maureen O'Hara, Natalie Wood and Edmund Gwenn. The running time is 93 minutes, and it's a delightful, nostalgic, well-written and humorous story, so grab a snack, or provide some treats for your friends, settle down, relax, and prepare to be entertained.

You may also wish to view the 1994 version, which is 109 minutes long and stars Richard Attenborough. Truthfully, I found it rather heavier and sadder than the original in tone. I have only referred to it in four places in this book, so it isn't totally necessary to view all of it during these studies, but I would recommend having it to hand because the different twist at the end of the court scene is significant, and I have chosen to use that in these studies rather than the (in my opinion) weaker courtroom conclusion in the 1947 version.

Along with the theme of faith, the film has obvious parallels with the story of Jesus, which are interesting to pull out and observe. You will probably see them as you watch the movie.

In brief, the story is about an elderly man, Kris Kringle, who is employed by Macy's store on 34th Street, New York, to play Santa Claus in the Thanksgiving Parade (after the original Santa is found to be intoxicated) and then in-store. The kindly old man seems to believe he really *is* Santa, and people love him. He even sends people to other shops to get the goods Macy's can't supply. This benevolent action actually enhances Macy's reputation, and Kris Kringle is soon seen as a major asset to the store.

Kris has been employed by Mrs Doris Walker, whose young daughter, Susan, has been very affected by her mother's bitter disappointment in a failed marriage. Mrs Walker is, at first, a brittle character, but it isn't long before she starts to warm to Kris Kringle.

However, not everyone likes the affable Kris, including the pseudo-psychologist Granville Sawyer, and Kris soon finds his sanity called into question.

Tricked, Kris is hospitalized. A court hearing ensues to determine whether or not he should be certified. But … could he really *be* Santa Claus? A cut-and-dried case seems more complicated than at first supposed. Kris is defended by attorney Fred Gailey, a genuine 'good guy' who is romantically interested in Mrs Walker. And at the end of the film, it seems that Kris may actually be who he claimed to be after all … It's a feel-good film, thought-provoking, uplifting and inspirational.

Incidentally, there are some features in the movie that truly date it. For instance, you might note that Mr Gailey – before he has even met Mrs Walker – is happily entrusted with the lone care of Susan (the 1994 version says she is six years old), a mark of more innocent times. And when Mrs Walker arrives to collect her daughter, Mr Gailey openly admits to wanting to meet the mother by befriending the child, which probably appears quite unacceptable to us today. You will very likely notice other issues which denote the age of the film – not least the mode of dress; personally, I love the formality of it.

The DVD cover of the 1994 version talks about 'something to believe in'. But Christmas, like Christianity, isn't about believing in 'something' – it's about believing in 'Someone'. It's about trusting the one who said he was the way, the truth, and the life (John 14:6). And Advent is the season where we think about waiting for and then celebrating the birth of this Christ-child. So it can be seen as a time of preparation, not for the secular trappings of a holiday, but for the arrival of Someone who will change hearts and lives where they are willing to be changed — not just 2,000 years ago, but today. It's about considering the implications of the coming of God-made-flesh ... for you. For me.

Whether you read the book in a group or on your own, my hope is that you come away from these studies with a greater sense of the reality and presence of the God who loves you. And that your faith in Jesus is sparked, or increased.

Sheila Jacobs
Halstead, Essex, 2015

WEEK ONE
Seeds of Faith

Group icebreaker

Have some seeds to hand – for example, nasturtium, marigold, runner bean, apple, tomato, pumpkin, a conker, an acorn, sunflower, a seasonal pine cone. Ask the group to identify the seeds. If you have a large enough group, this can be done in pairs. If you would like to award a small prize to the person/pair who have most right answers, do so. (You could make sure this prize can be shared; chocolate is always a good idea.) Ask them to think about the person or people who dropped seeds of faith into their lives. When and where did this happen? Share if you have time.

On your own

Think about the person or people who encouraged you to have faith in God (or perhaps gave you this book). Construct a letter of thanks to send or email later. If that isn't possible, keep the letter and thank God for the seeds of faith that were dropped into your life.

To start

Miracle on 34th Street is a film about a man who claims to be someone that sensible adults do not believe in – Santa Claus. Although he looks and acts the part and never deviates from his claim, the grown-up view is that this can't possibly be so. Santa is for children alone; a fantasy; not real life. Someone you believe in when you are young, but grow out of.

Our faith in God can be like this. If we were brought up to believe as children, we may find our faith is simply a reflection of our parents' own beliefs; or perhaps, as one person said to me, 'That Jesus stuff is okay when you're a kid, but we all grow up.' And it is true that it is as we grow up that we must make a decision for ourselves. Some people lose interest in Jesus; perhaps the challenges of a Christian lifestyle are just not appealing. But some choose to be baptized as an acknowledgement of their personal trust in Christ, and decide to follow him. In other traditions, people may be confirmed, acknowledging that they have come to believe for themselves the promises made for them as infants in respect of faith.

What do we mean by 'personal faith', for a Christian? It's simply this. We believe the claims that Jesus made about himself – who he is, and what he has done for us – and respond to him on a personal level. It has been said that God has no grandchildren. We cannot believe ourselves 'saved', heading for heaven and right with God just because our parents or grandparents are believers. We have to make a decision about Jesus for ourselves.

Of course, many people are not brought up in believing homes of any tradition. They may not even think about attending church. You might be one of these people. Perhaps you came to faith when you were older (as I did), or maybe you are on the journey, still exploring. Whichever applies to you, the way we were brought up will obviously strongly affect what we believe – certainly what we believe about God. And if we have children, or grandchildren, we must also be aware of the effect of our words and actions on *them*. Are we leading them into faith in Jesus? Are we accurately showing his love, making him the centre of our homes and lives? If not, would we like to?

PAUSE FOR THOUGHT

Think about your own coming to faith. If you have never come to a personal faith in Jesus, think of someone who has. Can you talk to them this week about their relationship with God through Christ?

Watch: 7:35 - 11:22

Kris Kringle has taken the place of the original inebriated Santa and is in the Thanksgiving Parade. Attorney Fred Gailey is watching the parade from his apartment window, accompanied by his neighbour's child, Susan.

Mr Gailey has an in-depth talk with the child about fantasy figures and very quickly discovers that her mother's views have taken firm root in the precocious

Susan. He finds out that she has never met her father – her parents divorced when she was a baby. Evidently the effect of Mrs Walker's hurt over the failed relationship has been transferred to the child. She has taught Susan not to believe in any kind of fantasy – 'No Santa Claus, no fairy tales, no fantasies of any kind,' as Fred Gailey asserts – to protect her.

PAUSE FOR THOUGHT

Do you think it right that Susan isn't allowed to believe in fantasies? Do you think a child being encouraged to believe in fairy tales as reality is harmful, or not?

EXTRA

If you have the new version of the film, watch 38:47 – 40:14.

Kris Kringle, Santa, the 'symbol of the season', tells Mrs Walker: 'You don't believe in me' and she replies that 'Christmas is for children', although she has in fact influenced her own child not to believe. How do you view Kris Kringle's statement that we are doomed to 'a life dominated by doubt' if we can't accept anything on faith?

Think about

Faith is a confident assurance or belief in a person or a thing.

We all have faith in *something*. Even if it isn't faith in Jesus, we may have faith in other people, our communities, our abilities, ourselves. I have heard people say, 'I trust nobody but myself. I can only rely on me.' Sadly, 'me' can prove just as untrustworthy as A. N. Other. We are all capable of making decisions that are based on selfish desires, self-centred principles and wrong ideas and information, and live to regret it.

We tend to lose faith – the element of trust – when we are let down. Our security is lost; the thing we relied on cannot be relied on anymore. Our definitions of what it means to trust are challenged. This can bring a great sense of loss, of fear, even of panic and emptiness. That is why it is so important to place our trust in something that is utterly reliable. However, many times we cannot know for sure what *is* reliable, and we must therefore first take that all-important step of faith. For example, if we choose to enter into marriage, we must exercise faith in our partner, trusting they will maintain their commitment to the vows they have made to us. But we cannot be *sure* they will be faithful. And if they prove not to be, it is not easy for trust to be regained.

Mrs Walker does not want her child to believe in fantasies. But sometimes *reality* takes a step of faith to believe in – when it is unseen. The initial step of faith in God is placing trust in Someone we cannot see, cannot touch, and cannot hear with our physical ears. And yet, as we move into relationship with God, we will begin to see the reality of the unseen in all manner of ways.

If we choose not to get married, because we fear our future partner might cheat on us, then our lack of trust means we will never take that leap of faith. Sometimes we will just have to take a chance if we are to find out, to our great delight, that our faith is not misplaced after all.

PAUSE FOR THOUGHT

Who do you really trust? If your answer is, 'No one', why is that?

Watch 18:46 – 24:23

Fred Gailey takes the unbelieving Susan to see Santa in Macy's store. He tells her: 'When you talk to him you might feel differently about him.'

Susan meets Kris Kringle but it's clear that she still doesn't believe in him. Commenting on his very real-looking beard, Kris invites Susan to 'Go ahead, pull it!' The first seed of faith is dropped in when Susan realizes that the beard isn't fake.

However, Mrs Walker arrives and squashes the first step of faith. Kris may be a 'nice old man' and 'those whiskers are real too' but that doesn't make him Santa Claus. Mrs Walker admonishes Fred Gailey; she is worried about Susan's mental health, being surrounded by 'gullible children' and meeting a 'convincing old man with real whiskers': 'What is she going to think? Who is she going to believe?' she asks. At this point Mrs Walker reveals her disappointment with real life. She doesn't want her child to grow up believing fantasies rather than reality – as she has evidently done herself. Fred Gailey asserts that 'We were talking about Susie, not about you'.

Susan slips away and watches Kris speaking to a little orphan Dutch girl in her own language, causing the seed of faith in Susan to begin to grow. Susan speaks to her mother about this, but her mother responds negatively. She asks Kris to tell Susan the truth because her daughter always wants to know 'the absolute truth' and he replies: 'Good, because I always tell the absolute truth.'

PAUSE FOR THOUGHT

What do you think of the worldview that says 'That may be true for you, but it isn't true for me'?

Think about

It is worth trying to remember our first steps of faith. We may have received wholly positive affirmation, but more likely we met with at least a little opposition along the way. We have to remember that people respond from their own experience. The people who may have poured cold water on our newly found faith probably had a negative faith history themselves ... and so we need to forgive, let it go, and nurture the seed rather than let it die.

All kinds of influences throughout our lives, before we know Christ for ourselves, can really affect our thinking. My granny was a 'born again Christian'. Her faith really matured when she was older. I had believed in God since an early age but only recall going to church about four times, twice as a teenager, and when I was obliged to by my school. However, I was really thinking about issues of faith by the time I was in my early 20s, due to the sudden death of a close friend. At a time when life wasn't very good, my granny came to stay and we found ourselves in a Christian bookshop, where I bought a book called *I Dared to Call Him Father* by Bilquis Sheikh. What really impressed me was that the author knew Jesus *personally.* I remember thinking, 'If this is possible, I want it.' That's when I asked Jesus to come into my life, even though I didn't understand much about what this meant. But I knew, as I got up off my knees, that I had 'met him' for myself.

My thoughts about Jesus were coloured by my granny's witness. There was 'something about her' that was just *different.* I see now, many years later, how that influenced my thinking. At any rate, I was open to reading the book I found in the Christian shop, and it helped my journey to faith.

How important it is to maintain a good witness in our families; especially when they don't know Jesus.

PAUSE FOR THOUGHT

How have your views of Jesus been coloured by other people's thoughts, teaching or example? How different might you feel if you met him, one to one?

Watch 14:14 – 15:18

The head of the toy department, Julian Shellhammer, gives Kris a list of toys Macy's store has to 'push'. Kris reacts against this – making the children take something they don't want because the store has bought too many of the wrong toys doesn't seem right to him. Kris talks about it to 17-year-old Alfred, who is sweeping up. Alfred says: 'There's a lot of bad "isms" floating around this world, but one of the worst is commercialism. Make a buck, make a buck … Don't care what Christmas stands for, just make a buck, make a buck.'

PAUSE FOR THOUGHT

Alfred has strong views on the time of year. What do you think Christmas 'stands for'?

Think about

Christmas has increasingly become a time when the values of materialism far outweigh the 'season of good will'. But the run-up to 25 December, the season we call Advent, should not be about 'making a buck'. It would seem it is, however, if we view it with purely secular eyes. It is worth thinking about what secular values actually are and mean. As we think about the commercialization of the season, we need to also see the bigger picture. What does our attitude to Christmas say about our belief system ... what exactly is society trusting in for happiness? One glance at the television shows us the standards and expectations which are the norm today.

Humanity is made to worship God. If we don't worship God, we will worship something else. That's when 'things' can become too important. Life becomes full of what we have or think we need. Our material status begins to define us. And if we lose it, often we feel we are losing our identity.

What saddens me, and perhaps it saddens you too, is the way young people in particular are so taken in by the trinkets of the world, and its cold values of 'how much money you've got', 'where you live', 'what you wear' and especially these days, 'how you look'. Basing relationships on superficial attraction that does not last has led to much heartache. And basing lives on the gathering of material goods we can never keep is pointless (see Luke 12:13-21). How shallow and damaged our society has become. And yet, when I was younger, before I met Christ and probably, realistically, for a while after, I had the same values. What about you?

When I was in my teens, I really, *really* wanted a high-achieving husband, a jeep, a horse, an Aga and a big farmhouse and fields to go with it. Status meant a great deal. I wanted to mix with 'the in-crowd', be seen with the right people, and look the part too. However, after a couple of crises, that dream swiftly crumbled. And now that I am older, I see that although material possessions are blessings and it is important to have enough money to pay the bills(!), it is far more important to have and know the presence of God, kindness and love. I am sure if I had a time machine and went back and told my 19-year-old self that little detail, I would be met with utter disbelief!

PAUSE FOR THOUGHT

How can we avoid some of the cynical attitudes that grow in us over the years in relation to Christmas?

EXTRA

If you have a copy of the 1994 version of the film, watch 51 – 52:19. Here, Mr Bedford

> *(the Fred Gailey character) is discussing Mrs Walker with Kris Kringle, after Mr Bedford has tried to propose to her. Think about how our own bitter attitudes can drag others into negativity. Are there any areas where God might be speaking to you about this?*

Watch: 28:18 – 28:59

'Christmas isn't just a day. It's a frame of mind.'

PAUSE FOR THOUGHT

Is the above statement true? In what ways is Christmas 'a frame of mind'?

THINK ABOUT

We continue in our thoughts about the secularization of Christmas. Although Kris Kringle is speaking here, these words might be a Christian plea. In truth, Jesus and the values of the kingdom of God are not just being pushed out of Christmas, but out of society itself. If we watch a lot of television, read many secular magazines and engage generally with the world, we will quickly find values that are at odds with the Bible.

This can be a challenge for mature believers as well as for those who are just starting to walk with Jesus. It is probably especially important for those of us who have followed Jesus for some time to maintain biblical values, to encourage those who have just begun to seek or follow him. We need to keep Jesus as our focus, and maybe examine ourselves to see if there are any areas of compromise which we have made that have diluted kingdom values in our own lives. Do we read magazines or watch things that we know are affecting our mind-set and worldview in a negative way? Do we entertain thoughts and values that we know are not biblical?

PAUSE FOR THOUGHT

Think on areas of your own life where God may be speaking to you about kingdom values.

Into Advent!

Read the 'I am' statements of Jesus:

> I am the bread of life. Whoever comes to me will never go hungry, and whoever believes in me will never be thirsty.
>
> (John 6:35)

> I am the light of the world. Whoever follows me will never walk in darkness, but will have the light of life.
>
> (John 8:12)

Very truly I tell you, I am the gate for the sheep.
All who have come before me are thieves and
robbers, but the sheep have not listened to them.
I am the gate; whoever enters through me will
be saved. They will come in and go out, and find
pasture.

(John 10:7-9)

I am the good shepherd; I know my sheep and
my sheep know me – just as the Father knows
me and I know the Father – and I lay down my
life for the sheep.

(John 10:14-15)

I am the resurrection and the life. The one
who believes in me will live, even though they
die; and whoever lives by believing in me will
never die. Do you believe this?

(John 11:25, 26)

I am the way and the truth and the life. No one
comes to the Father except through me.

(John 14:6)

I am the true vine, and my Father is the
gardener. He cuts off every branch in me that
bears no fruit, while every branch that does
bear fruit he prunes so that it will be even more
fruitful.

(John 15:1, 2)

Advent is a time of preparation; it is a time of hope. The coming of this King of kings is actually anticipated throughout history. Writing hundreds of years before Christ was born, the prophet Isaiah told of his birth (as well as what would happen to him). He said: 'The people walking in darkness have seen a great light' (Isaiah 9:2). This is Jesus, the Messiah, who would 'reign on David's throne' (Isaiah 9:7). Let's look further at this coming figure as described in Isaiah 9:6:

> For to us a child is born,
> to us a son is given,
> and the government will be on his shoulders.
> And he will be called
> Wonderful Counsellor, Mighty God,
> Everlasting Father, Prince of Peace.

In Micah 5:2 (NKJV) we read not only of exactly where the Saviour would be born, but also of his origins:

> But you, Bethlehem Ephrathah,
> Though you are little among the thousands of Judah,
> Yet out of you shall come forth to Me
> The One to be Ruler in Israel,
> Whose goings forth are from of old,
> From everlasting.

There's that word again – 'everlasting'. How interesting! The NIV (1984 version) footnote has:

'from days of eternity'. This was a divine person, as we read in Isaiah 7:14: 'Therefore the Lord himself will give you a sign: the virgin will conceive and give birth to a son, and will call him Immanuel.' 'Immanuel' means 'God with us'.

When Jesus used the 'I am' statements he was in effect speaking as deity (see Exodus 3:14; John 8:58). He made himself one with God, which is why the Jews wanted him dead (John 5:17-18). Many cults would say that he was not very God of very God. But while only a man could pay the price for humanity's sin, only God could live that life and lay it down as a sacrifice of infinite worth. Humanity suffers from the effect of the Fall. We couldn't save ourselves.

In John 14:6 Jesus says he is 'the way and the truth and the life. No one comes to the Father except through me'. When Kris Kringle says he tells the absolute truth, we might say this is exactly what Jesus is proclaiming here. But more than that, Jesus says he *is* the truth.

Susan starts to take baby steps in faith when she begins to think Kris might indeed be who he says he is – because he fits the image of Santa Claus, with his kindness and whiskers. Jesus 'fits the bill' of deity as we look into his life. His lifestyle backed up his claims. We begin to see the reality of the faithfulness of Jesus as we take small steps of faith. But as we travel on our journey, we must make sure to fix our eyes on him alone. Kingdom values that seem exciting and new when we first believe may prove costly as we attempt to implement them. It isn't easy to 'go God's way' in a secular world.

PAUSE FOR THOUGHT

- *Why is it important to acknowledge the deity of Christ?*
- *Can you think of any other verses that explicitly tell us of Christ's deity?*
- *What are some of the ways in which Jesus revealed his deity to the people he met?*

ACTIVITY SUGGESTIONS

- Light an Advent candle, and thank God for Jesus, the light coming into the world.
- Read aloud Isaiah 9:6:

> For to us a child is born,
> to us a son is given,
> and the government will be on his shoulders.
> And he will be called
> Wonderful Counsellor, Mighty God,
> Everlasting Father, Prince of Peace.

How do the names of Jesus here denote his deity?

FOR DISCUSSION

- Discuss Doris Walker's statement: 'I think we should be realistic and completely truthful with our children and not have them growing up believing in a lot of legends and myths like Santa Claus, for example.'
- How would you answer someone who denied that without belief in the deity of Christ, you cannot be a Christian?

REFLECTION

Reflect on Matthew 18:2,3: 'He called a little child to him, and placed the child among them. And he said: "Truly I tell you, unless you change and become like little children, you will never enter the kingdom of heaven."' Do you think it is really possible for an adult to come to Jesus like a little child? Why would he ask us to? Reflect on what a child is like when they come to someone they trust. What might coming to Jesus in a child-like way mean for you, personally?

PRAYER

Loving heavenly Father, as we begin this journey through Advent, let us keep in mind the real reason for the season. Thank you for those who have helped us this far in our getting to know you. Let us grow in faith as we walk through these studies, seeing you more clearly with every step, believing that the seed of faith planted in us can grow in the good soil of your love. Help us come to you as little children and to live to please you. Amen.

WEEK TWO
Friends and Enemies

Group icebreaker

How do you react when you are strongly challenged
on a personal level or on a view that is important to
you? Do you:

a) React with anger (storming out/arguing)
b) Act cool, but inside simmer with resentment
   ('I'll never speak to that person again!')
c) Ignore the opposition and dismiss their views
   ('They're just wrong. So what?!')
d) Listen, rejecting error but graciously receiving
   what might be true, even if challenging to you
   ('Okay, they may have a point, but I don't agree
   with x or y.')
e) Fall apart and feel as if someone has attacked
   your identity ('They hate me!')

Discuss.

On your own

Look at the Group icebreaker above. Think about
how you react to personal criticism or the criticism
of your values.

To start

Kris Kringle clearly believes he is Santa Claus. He asserts who he is, looks the part, acts the part, and never deviates from his claim. He shows integrity, and that is character strength.

What we believe about ourselves is important. If we believe we are worth nothing, no good, not only will that affect our own self-esteem but it will affect the perception of those who interact with us. Unfortunately, many of us may have experienced negative input regarding our very personalities, especially when we were young, and have a hard job throwing off the identity that others may have laid upon us. We need to see ourselves, therefore, as we really are – people God loves so much that he sent his Son to die for us.

Alternatively, we can have an overinflated view of ourselves. A lot of people these days refer to themselves as 'good': 'I'm a good person.' If you push that thought, they will protest, 'Well, I have never murdered anyone!' Goodness is relative, it would seem. But we have to face facts if we are seeking to be in relationship with the holy God.

The Bible tells us that we are sinners, and that all our good works are like filthy rags in his sight (Isaiah 64:6); we are naturally his enemies (Romans 5:10; Colossians 1:21). This is a truth some find hard to accept, but we can't get away from what the Word of God actually teaches. The great thing is that God loves us to much he has rescued us from ourselves. He did this when Jesus,

God incarnate (see John 1:1-18; Colossians 2:9; Hebrews 1:3) came to be born of Mary, to grow up living a perfect life that none of us could ever live, and laying that life down for us before being raised from the dead, proving his sacrifice was accepted by God and effective. Jesus was who he said he was; even more than his miracles, the resurrection proves that. He now intercedes for us with God the Father (Hebrews 7:25) and is coming back (Acts 1:11).

When Jesus died for us on the cross, he took the penalty of all the wrong things you and I have ever done to offend God and other people. More than that, he took away our old *nature* that was so corrupt, and gave us a new nature – his own – by the Holy Spirit who comes to live in us, giving us the power to please God. John 3:16 is the 'potted gospel': 'For God so loved the world that he gave his one and only Son, that whoever believes in him shall not perish but have eternal life.' It's not by works, it's by God's free, unmerited favour (Ephesians 2:8,9). This makes him our greatest Friend.

Jesus lived a life true to who he said he was. But integrity, as can be seen in the character and story of Kris Kringle, can bring enemies. Jesus had friends, and people who flocked to him, but there were some who were deeply challenged by his teaching and claims. Yet, against all opposition, he didn't waver. He didn't deny who he was, and his works were 'signs' of that, as John's Gospel tells us.

During Advent, while we are celebrating

the fact that Jesus came to earth, it is good to meditate on the reason he came. It was because we are all far from God and we need a Saviour; we need peace with God, a peace we can never achieve ourselves, by our own good works. And today, while many people are attracted to Jesus and accept him as their Saviour and the Lord of their lives, there are those who seek to persecute his followers. Yes, Jesus is our greatest Friend, but we must remember we also have an enemy, and we need to be on our guard against his wily devices (see Ephesians 6:10-18).

PAUSE FOR THOUGHT

Thank God for Jesus, who brought us peace with God!

Watch 30:35 – 34:19

In this clip, Kris manages to make an enemy of Granville Sawyer, Macy's resident 'psychologist' who examines employees. When Kris suggests that Mr Sawyer is exhibiting behaviour which would indicate he has hidden stress, Mr Sawyer reacts negatively. But the telephone conversation with his wife proves it to be true!

PAUSE FOR THOUGHT

During the Advent season, we don't often prepare so much for the coming King as the coming relatives. Mr Sawyer plainly has a stressful home life. Do you anticipate stressful situations this year? Are you able to share your concerns with God, and leave them with him?

Think about

Going back to the icebreaker, remember how you answered. Do you think our responses might depend on who it is who is challenging us? I can take on board personal criticism when it is delivered in love by someone I respect and who I believe wants the best for me. When criticism is levelled from someone who doesn't really know me (even if they think they do), I feel judged and defensive, even if they have a valid point.

God knows our hearts; he knows our innermost being, and our characters, inclinations and desires. So when he judges, he judges fairly. He understands our motivations and why we behave as we do. In Psalm 139:14 we read that we are 'fearfully and wonderfully made' – that surely means how we are made emotionally and psychologically, as well as physically.

PAUSE FOR THOUGHT

God knows everything about us, and yet loves us just the same. He knew each one of us before we were born (Jeremiah 1:5) and has witnessed everything we have ever said and done, yet he still sent his Son to save us. How might we respond to a God who loves us so unconditionally?

Watch 48:50 – 53:42

Here Kris discovers that Granville Sawyer is treating the ingenuous 17-year-old Alfred for mental complexes he does not believe Albert has. Threatening to tell Mr Macy, the boss, about the 'malicious contemptible fraud', he makes a further enemy of the 'meddling amateur', culminating in a very un-politically correct tap to the head with his cane!

This leads on to Mr Sawyer telling toy department manager Mr Shellhammer and Mrs Walker that when he attacked Kris' delusion of being Santa Claus, Kris became violent. Mr Sawyer is clearly acting vindictively. It is suggested that Kris sees a psychiatrist to ascertain whether he is mentally ill, and Mr Sawyer wants this examination to be carried out straight away (to protect himself).

But Mrs Walker won't tell Kris about this plan because she has grown fond of him. She thinks it is like telling Kris he is insane, and she won't do it. She does not want to hurt him.

PAUSE FOR THOUGHT

Sometimes it is easier to walk away from a difficult issue where we think we might hurt someone's feelings than it is to face the person in love, and deal with it. Mrs Walker's fondness for Kris is admirable. But do you think she handled this situation in the best way, given what happens next?

Think about

Love always protects (see 1 Corinthians 13:7). We can see this in Mrs Walker's refusal to hurt Kris. But we can see something else at work here, and it is deeply unpleasant. Granville Sawyer dislikes Kris Kringle because he feels attacked on a personal level – as well as by the cane. He also does not want Kris to complain to Mr Macy about him. So he manipulates and conspires to get rid of the problem.

Jesus was very unpopular with certain people – the religious leaders. This was because he confronted them on a personal level; basically, he exposed them as hypocrites and challenged their integrity. On many occasions they tried to stop him, catch him out, or kill him (see for example John 7:1,19). He admonished them (see

Matthew 23) and they didn't like it one bit. Their answer was to get rid of him; in their view, he was a troublemaker. They thought that if the people believed in Jesus, it would cause huge problems for the Jewish nation with the Roman occupiers of their land. In fact it was the high priest, Caiaphas, who said that 'it is better ... that one man die for the people than ... the whole nation perish' (John 11:45-52).

As well as being seen as a troublemaker, there were questions regarding Jesus' sanity. At one stage his family thought he was out of his mind, and some teachers of the law thought he was possessed by the devil (see Mark 3:20-22).

PAUSE FOR THOUGHT

How did Jesus react when challenged? How did he react on the cross?

Watch 53:44 - 55:33

Here we see the malevolence of Mr Sawyer at work as he influences Julian Shellhammer. The toy department manager is manipulated into lying to Kris. He says that Mrs Walker has asked him to tell Kris that some publicity pictures are going to be taken at city hall with the mayor. There is a car waiting outside ....

Of course, naïve Kris trusts Mr Shellhammer and is duped. He realizes this when Mr Sawyer gets into the car too. They are going to Bellevue (psychiatric) Hospital.

Kris asks whether Mrs Walker knew about the set-up. Mr Sawyer replies, 'Yes, we all discussed it.' But that wasn't actually true; this statement has a grain of truth mixed with a lot of untruth. Mrs Walker *didn't* know about the subterfuge. Mr Sawyer is twisting the truth and adding to it – much as we can see in the Genesis story of the Fall of humanity, when Eve, enticed by the enemy, added to the truth (see Genesis 3).

PAUSE FOR THOUGHT

It is easy to mix truth with falsehood, especially when we are tempted to manipulate difficult circumstances in our favour. How important is it to maintain our integrity, even if it costs us to do so?

Think about

While Mr Sawyer is plainly an enemy, Mr Shellhammer has hardly acted as a friend. He may have thought he was acting in the best interests of the store, but he has still lied. Sometimes we think 'little white lies' won't hurt. But the trouble is, they can lead to all kinds of other problems where we find ourselves led into larger and more elaborate fabrications to protect ourselves … Then our 'little white lie' becomes quite a big deal.

It is a sickening feeling when someone we trust lies to us and we find out. If this is a significant person in our life, it has the potential to be devastating. Even when the lie seems small, it can still leave a bad taste in the mouth and even alter our view of the person who has delivered it. Personally I would rather be told an unpalatable truth than swallow a sugar-coated lie, even if it takes me some time to process the thought and come to terms with it.

It is also very destructive when someone slanders another so that our opinion is warped or changed towards the person we hear about. Slander and gossip are so utterly damaging, and yet I suspect we have all engaged in it to some degree at some time or another.

Malicious talk and manipulative, controlling behaviour are the work of the enemy, and of our sinful nature. Tempted to indulge in it, we can destroy so much. Once lost, trust is a hard thing to regain, as we considered earlier.

PAUSE FOR THOUGHT

Have you been lied to by someone you had faith in? How has this affected your relationship with them?

Watch 56:22 - 57:34

Kris has failed the mental ability examination deliberately. He has become despondent about his friendship with Mrs Walker, believing she was just humouring him all along. But then Fred Gailey tells him that Mrs Walker wasn't part of the set-up. It was all Mr Sawyer's idea.

Mr Gailey explains that Mrs Walker didn't want to hurt Kris. But Kris says that Mrs Walker thought he was just 'a nice kind old man and she was sorry for me … She had doubts. That's why she was just sorry.'

'All right, she had doubts,' says Mr Gailey. 'Why not? She hasn't really believed in anything for years.'

PAUSE FOR THOUGHT

There is a difference between sympathy, where you may feel pity for someone else, and compassion, which motivates you to do something about the problem. Carry out a Bible search online or in a study Bible for the word 'compassion' and see how many times it is used about the character and nature of God.

Think about

This is a very interesting piece of the film because it presents us with so many ideas for question and debate.

1. Have you ever felt despondent and hopeless about a relationship, or about life itself?

2. Is feeling 'sorry' enough?
3. Is it okay to doubt – even doubt our faith, when we have believed for years?
4. What kinds of things shake our faith in God?
5. How do we reach people with the gospel when they haven't 'believed in anything for years'?

Let's take each of these points in turn. (If you are in a group, you may like to pick one.)

1. *Have you ever felt despondent and hopeless about a relationship, or about life itself?*
   Many of us have suffered the ending or collapse of a relationship, whether it involves a friend, colleague, family member, romantic partner/ spouse. Being without someone you have shared your life with in whatever capacity, or struggling to hold things together at a so-called 'happy' time of year, can be quite a strain. Christmas is heralded as a time of family togetherness, but that ideal is not always the case. Indeed, it can be a time when, hiding behind the façade of tinsel and turkey, many people find themselves struggling with feelings of great loneliness. It can be very hard time indeed for 'broken' families, especially when one parent or grandparents are not able to see as much of beloved children as they would like. When we are hurt, we can easily fall into depression and feel like giving up – as Kris Kringle does in the film. But there is *always* hope when we look to Jesus. Although things

don't always seem to go right, life is hard, and people let us down, God never will. It may feel as if he has; but that is where faith comes in. If God is good, and he is love (1 John 4:8), then we are invited to trust him with the outcome of whatever difficult situation we may find ourselves in. And remember, the God of compassion can change people *and* circumstances, even when we cannot.

2. *Is feeling 'sorry' enough?*

   It's okay to feel sorry, but it is another thing to do something about it. 2 Corinthians 7:10 tells us that 'Godly sorrow brings repentance that leads to salvation and leaves no regret, but worldly sorrow brings death'. When we are truly sorry, we 'repent'. That's an old-fashioned word. But it means to forsake the old way and live differently. It's taking a U-turn. It's going another way. I suspect we all know people who are trapped in sorrow because of some tragic event, and often, trapped in unforgiveness too. I think that is a kind of worldly sorrow; it brings spiritual death, and depressing of the senses. I have found that when I let God down, and try to hide my sin like Adam and Eve did in the Garden, I feel a certain separation from my Creator. It is only when I come and acknowledge my sin, with no excuses, in repentance, and ask for forgiveness and the power to change that I have a 'restored friendship' with God. Not that he has ceased to love me; no. I have just constructed a wall between us. Only repentance, acknowledging fault, can take that wall down. If we are truly sorry for our wrong thoughts and actions when we come to God, there will be a marked change in our lives. Otherwise … well; it's just words. We have to also remember that we need to forgive others, as the Lord forgives us (Colossians 3:13).

3. *Is it okay to doubt – even doubt our faith - when we have believed for years?*

There have been times in my adult life as a Christian when things have been really tough and I have questioned God. Not his existence – I know he's there; past experiences prove that! I suppose I have questioned his goodness, or at least his goodness to me, in light of some of my challenges. And yet I know he *is* good, and that he 'works for the good of those who love him' (Romans 8:28). It is only when looking back that we sometimes see the good that God has brought out of trying situations – and, marvelling at this, praise him for it. Note here that he doesn't promise to work things out for the good of those who do *not* love him. But God has broad shoulders. He can take our doubts; we can leave them safely with him. Maybe sometimes we should act in faith *even though* we doubt, and see what happens?

4. *What kinds of things shake our faith in God?*

All kinds of things may shake our faith in God

(and in people). It's usually when we have asked for help but not received it. We may question the goodness of God, or even his very existence, when we go through what has been called 'the dark night of the soul'. To be like Job, and say that 'The LORD gave and the LORD has taken away' and to add 'may the name of the LORD be praised' (Job 1:21) is a high point of faith. To praise God when all seems lost is to give glory to the Creator *despite* the circumstances. How pleased our heavenly Father must be when his children praise him during their doubts and disappointments, showing trust in who he is in the face of their trials and temptations. (It is worth carrying out a faith-enhancing Bible study in the names and attributes of God; maybe you can do that when you have finished this Advent course!)

5. *How do we reach people with the gospel when they haven't 'believed in anything for years'?*
   People can be immunized against the gospel by all manner of things, including wrong spiritual connections – i.e. involvement in the occult, teaching that has seemed to disprove humanity's need for a God even if God did exist, early negative influences about God, bad experiences of church – and yes, religious belief. Many people find it difficult to accept a gospel of grace (salvation as a free gift when you accept what Jesus has fully accomplished on the cross … nothing to be added!) because they have

so believed in a gospel of works. While works prove our faith (James 2:14-26), there is nothing we can add to the work of Christ so we might be saved. When I first met Jesus, I accepted salvation – I knew he was the only way I could be right with God. But then I felt I had to work like crazy almost to 'pay him back'. However, reading the book of Ephesians and the work of Watchman Nee in the excellent *Sit, Walk, Stand* (CLC) changed my view and I began to see that we have to rest in God to truly 'work' for him. I look at it this way: an elderly friend of mine has a stair lift, by which she can ascend the stairs much more quickly than she would in her own power. Seated, she can move. Get the picture? I heartily recommend you have a look at Ephesians 2:1-10 if you have time. How could we ever raise *ourselves* up, as we read in that passage, and seat *ourselves* with Christ? This is the love of God that he has 'lavished' on us (read Ephesians 1:7,8). How we need to reach people with this amazing good news of great joy that is heralded by the angels at Christmas-time!

PAUSE FOR THOUGHT

Have you seen the 'lavish' love of God for you yet? Is Christmas 'personal' for you? Do you really see God's grace as a gift, or do you still strive to 'work' for God?

Watch 57:34 – 59:03

Disheartened Kris Kringle asserts that Mr Sawyer is 'contemptible, dishonest, selfish, deceitful, vicious and yet he's out there and I'm in here. He's called normal and I'm not. Well, if that's normal, I don't want it'.

But as the visiting attorney Fred Gailey points out, it isn't just about Kris. He cannot simply think about himself. What happens to Kris matters 'to a lot of other people; people like me, who believe in what you stand for, and people like Susie who are just beginning to. You can't quit. You can't let them down'.

Kris then places his trust in Mr Gailey: 'You'll get me out of this. You'll think of something … I believe in you.'

PAUSE FOR THOUGHT

Is there anyone you trust as completely as Kris Kringle trusts Fred Gailey?

Think about

We read earlier that at one point, Jesus' own close family thought he was crazy. And as we look in the Bible, we can see that Jeremiah, Ezekiel, Elijah and John the Baptist were hardly displaying 'normal' behaviour at times! Anyway – what's 'normal'? These days, saying you believe a man who was killed 2,000 years ago is alive and coming back again seems … well, pretty radical.

I have been involved in street evangelism for a few years now, and for a time shared the gospel on Saturday evenings on the streets of a large town. While a great number of the young people we spoke to made fun of our beliefs and heckled the street preachers (whatever your view of street preaching, these guys were brave!), there were many who were hungry to hear about a God who loved them. We were fools for Christ (see 1 Corinthians 1:10), but knew we had something that could change the lives of these young people. Jesus.

It's hard to stand up for what you believe in. It's easy to give in, especially when you feel alone. We looked at kingdom values in Week One. In our own families, at work, it is difficult to live out those kingdom values when other people are living by a very different standard. Jesus said, 'In this world you will have trouble' (John 16:33), that 'broad is the road that leads to destruction' and that we should 'Enter through the narrow gate' (Matthew 7:13). I look at it this way. The broad road is beautifully smooth and smells of flowers. But it ends in a sheer drop that will kill you. The narrow gate leads to a stony path that is often difficult to navigate, and hurts to walk on at times. But it ends somewhere beautiful – which is worth getting to.

If we have been Christians for a while, we may be tempted to take some spiritual time off, relax and generally chill out. By taking spiritual time off, I mean we may stop bothering so much about 'God stuff'. We may decide to put the Bible away, and stop going to church or house groups. After all, we have busy lives and it is easier to lie in on a Sunday morning, or go to the shops, or catch up with all those little jobs we haven't got round to. Perhaps the sermons seem more tedious these days, and the fellowship a little stale. There's no excitement anymore. So where's the harm in letting it all go for a while?

Or we may think indulging in a little sin is no real problem; especially if we are jaded about our walk with Christ. If it's got old, or boring – watch out. We may think we are strong enough to handle our sin; it's no big deal, everybody's doing it, it won't hurt anybody in the end, we can stop whenever we like. What a dangerous place to be in! It's like putting your hand in the fire expecting not to get burned. If you say, 'I'm going to have some time off God but I'll be back in a few months/a year', beware. You may never come back at all.

Another reason we might hang up our spiritual clothes for a while may be because we have experienced a degree of persecution. In that case it is often easier to 'keep the peace' and give in to compromise. (See Hebrews 10: 26-29.)

Our enemy is very clever. Satan knows our weaknesses and can tempt us in all manner of ways, especially when we let things slide. Many church leaders have got into all kinds of sin and this has affected the faith of others. As mature believers, we have a responsibility to those who are just beginning to follow Jesus to maintain our integrity. The devil doesn't give up ... just because we are older, or have been Christians a long time doesn't mean we are immune from temptation and falling away. Far from it. We need to make sure we finish well for our own sakes – and also for the next generation. Many people who don't yet know Jesus, or who are just beginning on the road of discipleship, look to their elders in the faith for guidance and as role models, certainly at the very start of their journey. So, what we do matters.

And who we trust in and believe in matters too. I have a few very good trusted friends. Years ago, I was quite gullible and trusted anyone who called themselves 'Christian'. These days I am a little wiser. Even so, we are all just human. Ultimately, although we all need (and need to be) good role models for Jesus, we can only look to him for perfection. And we cannot live for him in our own strength. That will set us up for failure. We must remember that without him we can do nothing (see John 15:5). If we need strength, freedom from fear, release from apathy, whatever it is, we must go to him and ask him. He won't let us down (see Luke 11:11-13).

PAUSE FOR THOUGHT

In what (or in whom) do you put your trust ... really? Be honest!

Into Advent!

God's free favour was about to be shown to the earth. He was bringing about peace between humanity and himself. God, in Christ, was coming in the flesh to live with us (John 1:14). It isn't something we deserved or worked for. It's a gift. It's a gift we need and a gift we don't have to accept. But the fact is, we, like our first ancestors, are far from God in our fallen state. We need to be taken out of the kingdom of darkness and translated into the kingdom of God – we are redeemed, bought back from the grip of the enemy by our God who loves us (Ephesians 2:1,2), but we need to accept that gift for ourselves.

We can see the work of the enemy a little while after Jesus was born. The story of the Magi, or Wise Men, which can be found in Matthew 2:1-18, finishes with a heinous action by King Herod.

Although the Wise Men and their gifts of gold, frankincense and myrrh, denoting royalty, deity and death, are part of the traditional Nativity tale, they didn't arrive in Bethlehem probably until about two years after the child was born. The Bible tells us they were from 'the east' (Matthew 2:1), which could be Persia, or modern-day Iran. Stargazers, they had seen the sign in the heavens that a king of the Jews had been born (Matthew 2:2) and come to worship him, eventually arriving in Jerusalem. But the King they were looking for wasn't born in a palace.

King Herod, a non-Jew, was obviously threatened by this. He checked out biblical prophecies about where the Messiah, the long-awaited Saviour of the Jews, would be born, and discovered it was Bethlehem (Matthew 2:6). He therefore attempted to deceive the Magi. He sent them to Bethlehem, and said that as soon as they found the child they should tell him, so he could worship him too. But of course, that wasn't what he intended to do at all.

The Magi found Jesus, following the star that 'stopped over the place where the child was' (Matthew 2:9). They proved they were indeed wise when they heeded a warning in a dream not to return to Herod.

When King Herod discovered they had outsmarted him, he was furious and killed all the boys in Bethlehem of two years and under. But Joseph, Jesus' stepfather, after an angelic visitation in another dream, had been warned that Herod was going to try to kill Jesus, and the family had escaped to Egypt.

The enemy didn't give up throughout Jesus' lifetime – and he doesn't give up on us either. We have to be very aware not to let him destroy our lives, our ministries. We need to stay close to Jesus.

PAUSE FOR THOUGHT

- *How did Herod act when threatened?*
- *What might have happened if the Wise Men had trusted Herod (see Matthew 2:12)?*
- *Why does humankind need a Saviour who is both man and God? Who is our real enemy?*

ACTIVITY SUGGESTIONS

- Read some literature or look at websites which deal with the persecuted church, e.g. www. opendoorsuk.org or www.releaseinternational. org. How might you or your group help to support those who are suffering?
- Think of friends you know you can really trust. This Christmas, could you say thank you to them in a special way? It doesn't need to be by way of an expensive present. Spend time thinking about this. If you are in a group that you really appreciate, perhaps you could arrange a special treat for the new year – a shopping trip, a meal together.

FOR DISCUSSION

- 'You'll get me out of this. You'll think of something … I believe in you.' These are Kris Kringle's words to Fred Gailey. Are they ever our words to God? And if they are, what happens – or has happened?
- How important is it that we put our faith in the right people, or things? What can happen when we don't?

REFLECTION

It is when we forgive that we are forgiven. Is there anyone you need to say sorry to? A person … the Lord? Do you need to forgive an enemy? Can you think about praying for someone you would not consider a good friend … or even very likeable?

PRAYER

Dear loving heavenly Father
How good you are that you love us so much that you sent your one and only Son to come to save us, and give us peace with you. Thank you for this Advent season, when we are remembering how Jesus came, and why. Help us to remember you and find your peaceful presence in the middle of all the busyness.

Father, we have friends for whom we thank you, but we also have an enemy, so please help us be constantly aware, and stand firm in our faith in Jesus, keeping faithful to you.
Amen.

WEEK THREE
When Common Sense Tells You Not To

Group icebreaker

Have a Christmas cracker, and throw it to each
other, with the question: 'Have you ever done
anything when common sense has told you not
to? What happened?' If you can't think of an
answer, throw it to the next person. Only stop
throwing the cracker when you have exhausted
all the answers.

On your own

Have you ever done anything (or bought anything!)
on the spur of the moment, and regretted it?
Alternatively, have you ever decided not to take a
risk, but later wished that you had?

To start

In the court scene, Kris Kringle never deviates
from his claim. He asserts that he is Santa Claus.
Is he crazy? Deluded? Or could he *really* be Father
Christmas?

During the Advent season, we are remembering
the coming of God incarnate into our world. We
have said it is a time of preparation, as we think
about celebrating the birth of God's Son. But as
we consider the coming of Jesus, we look forward,
too, to the second coming, when Christ will be

revealed not as a baby, this time, but as the victorious King. And we may be reminded that the child grew up to die a horrendous death on the cross.

It's easy at this time of year to think of the rather cute manger scene portrayed by little children in Nativity plays. In a way, baby Jesus is a safe Jesus. He doesn't challenge us. He doesn't ask us tough questions or demand anything from us. At Christmas, Jesus is a happy baby asleep in a crib, with a sweet mother and protective stepfather, surrounded by adoring animals and assorted shepherds, with angels and Wise Men completing the scene. But anyone who has been a Christian for a while will soon tell you that following Jesus isn't a fairy tale. We face all kinds of trials and – perhaps in this country, comparatively minor – persecutions. But it can be very difficult to make choices to honour God in a society (and perhaps a family) that doesn't.

Believers' views, changed over time to line up with the Word of God, are very much at odds with much of today's world. We make absolute claims that can upset people. Jesus told us that he was the only way to God (John 14:6). That's difficult for some people to hear, when they think that there are many paths to the divine. New Age beliefs – a kind of pick 'n' mix spirituality – can lead to a sort of 'make up your own religion that suits your way of life'. To look at the claims of Jesus and begin to follow him, saying 'your will, not mine', is a tall order for many living in an individualistic, independent world.

Jesus was arrested on trumped-up charges because the religious leaders believed him to be dangerous. In the film, Kris Kringle is referred to as being a 'menace to society' (01.10:47) and that's the way Jesus was viewed, too. Being a Christian *is* dangerous – especially in many parts of the world which experience true persecution, as we have seen in Week Two's Activity Suggestions. If we live for Jesus, we won't always be popular and will have to make decisions others may think ridiculous or weird. For example, in prayer, we may hear God telling us to give up a good job to train to become a missionary in a poor part of the world. Or we may feel God is asking us to give up a relationship with someone we like or even hoped to marry. To obey God is to take a leap of faith.

To really trust anyone, you have to really know them. I have some friends who have stuck with me through thick and thin, and I believe they love me. How do I know that? Because they say so? No. Because they *act* so ... consistently.

Jesus acted consistently throughout his earthly life. He made extraordinary claims, as we saw earlier. Apart from saying he was the only way to God – an enormous and absolutely outrageous claim, unless it was true – he said: 'I am the resurrection and the life' (John 11:25). *He is* the resurrection? Yet he proved it effectively, when he raised people from the dead – and rose himself.

I am sure you can think of instances of 'impossibilities' during the earthly ministry of Jesus – changing water into wine, for example (John 2). Doing 'whatever he says' (verse 5), against all common reasoning, however unlikely, can certainly deepen our faith when we see astonishing results. If Jesus asks us to come to him walking on the water – whatever that might mean in our own circumstances – it may take a great deal of faith to step out of the boat, but to do so will be for our ultimate benefit as well as to the glory of God (Matthew 14:22-33).

When Jesus was on trial before Pontius Pilate, he stayed silent in accordance with the Scriptures (see Isaiah 53:7). But when he did speak, he did not deviate from his initial claim. He said he was a king, and that discourse provoked the famous 'What is truth?' response from Pilate (John 18:38; read John 18:28-38).

Throughout his earthly ministry, Jesus was asking people to put their faith in him. John 14:1 exhorts us: 'You believe in God; believe also in me.' It must have been very hard indeed for the disciples to see the one they believed in arrested, charged and then crucified. But that was before the resurrection. Jesus had said he would rise again (e.g. Matthew 16:21), but resurrection at that time must have seemed impossible. One of my favourite miracles of Jesus is the extraordinary catch of fish we read about in John 21. Fishing all night with nothing to show for it, Jesus tells the disciples to try again – mirroring an earlier episode (see Luke 5:1-11) and showing that it was him, himself; he really was alive.

To follow Jesus you have to believe in him, trust in him, and obey him. It's when we take a risk and step out in faith that we see God at work. It's when we trust him that he rewards us. It's when we obey him – whatever the cost – that we see the precious Lord truly guiding and leading us for our good and his glory.

PAUSE FOR THOUGHT

Have you ever taken a real risk for Jesus? What was it, and what happened?

EXTRA

In the 1994 version, if you have it, watch 01.17 – 01.17:50. In this brief clip, Mrs Walker is talking to Mr Bedford, the updated Fred Gailey character. She has rather brutally refused his proposal of marriage and admits here to being scared. Fear stops us doing things; it can prevent us from taking risks. Is fear stopping you from taking a risk right now?

Watch 01.03:50 – 01.07:37

Kris Kringle confidently tells the court who he is. Interestingly, Fred Gailey offers some challenging words. Normally it would be absurd for anyone to claim to be Santa Claus – unless he really is. Then the claim becomes true.

If someone else claimed to be me, I would conclude that they were deluded – or up to no good. We could call it 'identity theft'. But when I claim to be me, because I am, that's fine!

PAUSE FOR THOUGHT

Think of the 'I am' claims of Jesus we read in Week One. Do you think he was deluded, up to no good – or telling the truth?

Think about

When we think about identity, what comes to mind? People can lose their sense of identity when they get heavily immersed in a lifestyle choice that overwhelms them. All kinds of addiction can make a person lose their very 'self' as they are taken over by something they ultimately cannot control. And sometimes, people simply reject who they are. They don't like their true identities. They would rather be someone else.

It is often easier to opt for a fantasy version of ourselves. Perhaps we'd like to be 'just like … ' (name your favourite TV, music or movie star). The celebrity culture is increasingly upon us. But of course, even the 'star' we would like to emulate isn't actually the 'perfect' person often portrayed by the media. Reality crashes in when we see past the shiny exterior. I am sure you can think of 'celebs' who met an untimely end – Marilyn Monroe, Elvis Presley, Jim Morrison, Kurt Cobain, River Phoenix, Heath Ledger, Amy Winehouse, Robin Williams … Sadly, Natalie Wood, who plays Susan in this film, died in a drowning incident at the age of forty-three.

Facebook is a hugely popular way of spending time and sharing ourselves with the world. But how much of it is reality? Beautiful photos, the glossy life … I know of people who get quite depressed reading how amazing other people's lives seem to be, as they are represented on social media. 'My life isn't like that at all!' they wail. I suspect they are victims of a kind of identity fraud. We want to portray our best self, looking good and enjoying the finest life. But it isn't always real.

When we come to Christ, we are 'born again' (see John 3:3-8). After Jesus died and was raised from the dead, he returned to his heavenly Father and sent the Spirit of God so that his followers would have the power to live for him. In effect, this new birth makes us 'new creations' (2 Corinthians 5:17). What does that mean? It means that our old self is crucified with Christ; we died with him, and our sin is atoned for. Raised into new life with him, we are new creatures. The Spirit of God begins to make us like Jesus – the fruit being the 'love, joy, peace, patience, kindness, goodness, faithfulness, gentleness and self-control' we read about in Galatians 5:22 (NIV, 1984).

As we begin to walk with him, we will find our 'old nature' is at odds with the new nature in Christ. But our true identity, as we read in Ephesians, is in Jesus (Ephesians 2:1-16). We no longer have to prove or re-invent ourselves, or wish we were someone else – a better version of 'me'. We are sons and daughters of the living God, loved and accepted for who we are. There is a real security when we truly know who God is, and who we are. The book of Galatians tells us: 'But when the set time had fully come, God sent his Son, born of a woman, born under the law, to redeem those under the law, that we might receive adoption to sonship' (Galatians 4:4,5). Sonship! God is our Father.

If we know Jesus and have asked him to be our Saviour, acknowledging him as Lord of our life, we have a whole new identity. Whatever label the world wants to give us, we are children of a heavenly kingdom, a kingdom that is not of this world (John 17:16). We are 'aliens and strangers' (1 Peter 2:11, NASB), just passing through. Do you believe that?

PAUSE FOR THOUGHT

Have you ever really seen your true identity in Christ? How does thinking about yourself as a son or daughter of the living God affect you with regard to your actions and identity?

Watch 01.7:37 - 01.10

During this powerful conversation, Fred Gailey tells Mrs Walker that he has given up his job to defend Kris Kringle. He says, 'I can't let Kris down. He needs me.' Doris Walker admires him for wanting to help Kris, but thinks he should be 'realistic and face facts' and that he shouldn't throw his career away 'for a sentimental whim'.

Mr Gailey asks her to 'believe in me and have faith in me'. But then he realizes that she doesn't believe in him. He says: 'You don't have any faith in me, do you?' and Mrs Walker replies, 'It's not a question of faith, it's just common sense.' Mr Gailey then answers with a wonderful definition of faith: 'Faith is believing in things when common sense tells you not to.'

Fred Gailey says that Kris Kringle stands for 'kindness and joy and love and all the other intangibles'. Doris Walker's reply could be said of those who doubt the Christian faith: 'You're talking like a child; you're living in a realistic world and those lovely intangibles of yours are attractive but not worth very much.' She says, 'You don't get ahead that way.' Mr Gailey and Mrs Walker obviously have very different life values; he doesn't see 'getting ahead' the way that she does. She says he is on an 'idealistic binge', having thrown away his job and 'security'. Then he answers that one day she may discover that these intangibles are 'the only things that are worthwhile'.

PAUSE FOR THOUGHT

Where is your 'security'? In your job? Your marriage? In God?

Think about

This is a very interesting part of the film, because it shows how very different Fred Gailey's mind-set is from that of his love interest. At first glance it would look as if Mrs Walker is right in what she says. Throwing a good job away would seem a foolish move. But when your values are compromised, what do you do? Well … you make a choice.

Walking on the water (mentioned above) was, for the disciple Peter, a remarkable step of faith. Mrs Walker, in the same position, I believe, at this stage of the film, would have given Jesus all the reasons why she shouldn't get out of the boat. Mr Gailey may well have taken the step of faith and chosen to jump over the side – and found his personal faith in Jesus grow enormously as a result.

Being a Christian is often about getting out of the boat when we would rather not. But sometimes it is just impossible to stay in that boat. If something or somewhere is becoming uncomfortable for us, it might be God stirring us up to challenge us to move on in him.

Finding our security in Jesus, finding he is faithful to his promises as we obey him, leads to peace. Indeed, every step of faith leads us closer to God.

However, we have to make sure of the voice we are listening to. When we feel we are being led in a certain direction, we must ask, 'Is it really God I am hearing?' Jesus said we would hear his voice if we are his sheep (see John 10:1-16). He guides and protects us, telling us 'This is the way; walk in it' (Isaiah 30:21). It is up to us to obey.

There are times in life when we don't really know what to do. We may pray for guidance and still not feel totally sure we have heard from God. In those cases, we need to just 'do it'. There are other times when we might 'hear' something that is manifestly against the Word of God and yet want to act on it. It could be that we want something (or someone!) that we know God does not want us to have, and we block our ears to his voice – to our own harm. Let's ask God for more discernment and the boldness and courage to obey him; let's trust that he really does know best and loves us so much that he doesn't want us to go wrong.

We can so easily fix our eyes and hearts on things – or people – that will hurt us, and others. Perhaps it is only as we have been walking with Jesus for a while that we will see the truth that some things are more important than the things many of the people of this world value and esteem … the materialism, for a start, that we see flooding our shopping centres, and in magazines and on TV in the Advent season.

Into Advent!

Read Luke 2:1-20.

As anyone who has ever attended a traditional
Nativity play knows, Jesus was born in Bethlehem;
his parents had to go there to register because of
a census of the Roman world. Mary's soon-to-be
husband, Joseph, was living in Nazareth, but he
came from the lineage of King David, and Bethlehem
was the town of David; everyone had to register in
their home town, so that was where Mary and Joseph
had to go.

Baby Jesus arrived during that time, and was
laid in a feeding trough. There was 'no room for
[Mary and Joseph] in the inn' (KJV) so it seems
they were staying where the animals were housed.

Interestingly, the first people to be called to
witness the arrival of the Saviour of the world were
those who at the time would have been considered
people with little status – the shepherds.

It is fascinating to read the angels' promise.
After telling the shepherds not to be afraid, they
said they had come to bring good news that would
bring great joy. Joy! How exciting!

It seems the shepherds didn't question their own sanity or choose to disbelieve the heavenly messengers who announced, 'Glory to God in the highest heaven, and on earth peace to those on whom his favour rests' (Luke 2:14). Instead, the shepherds, having witnessed the heavenly chorus in the fields, decided to follow angelic direction (verse 12) and take a look for themselves.

That's the way to start the journey to personal belief. People might tell us of their own faith. They might hope we believe – just as Fred Gailey clearly would like Doris Walker to believe. But it is only when we 'check out' the claims of Christianity and encounter Christ for ourselves that we see the truth. I came to faith partly through reading the testimony of someone who had met with Jesus herself. I saw then that this was possible, and I too wanted that relationship. However, if I had never had an encounter with Jesus for myself, it would all still be theoretical.

In the Christian life, we follow a Saviour who was born in a stable building, and who grew up to serve and to die. He said that we should be humble (see e.g. John 13:14; Luke 14:7-11) as he was humble – as we see in Philippians 2:6-11. Here we read of Jesus

> Who, being in very nature God,
> did not consider equality with God something to
> be used to his own advantage;
> rather, he made himself nothing

by taking the very nature of a servant,
being made in human likeness.
And being found in appearance as a man,
he humbled himself
by becoming obedient to death –
even death on a cross!
Therefore God exalted him to the highest place
and gave him the name that is above every
name,
that at the name of Jesus every knee should bow,
in heaven and on earth and under the earth,
and every tongue acknowledge that Jesus Christ is
Lord,
to the glory of God the Father.

Being a Christian and holding on to your status is
pretty impossible. Following Jesus is the antithesis
to 'getting ahead'.

PAUSE FOR THOUGHT

- *Have you ever thought about the coming of
  Jesus as 'good news' for you personally?*
- *Do you experience joy in your relationship
  with Jesus – or has serving him become
  lifeless and boring?*
- *Why not ask God to give you a fresh
  revelation of his good news for you today?*

ACTIVITY SUGGESTIONS

- Can you write a card, email, text, phone or find time to squeeze in a visit to someone who needs to know the kindness, joy and love of Jesus this Advent season?
- Is there someone you are hoping will come to faith this Christmas? If you are in a group, think of some different ways to perhaps encourage loved ones (and others!) to know Christ for themselves. More than words, sometimes, just living in obedience to Christ can prompt questions about what makes Christians 'different'. Share brief testimonies, if you have time. If you are on your own, jot some ideas down and spend time asking God how to pray for the person/people you care about.

FOR DISCUSSION

- How does knowing our identity in Christ strengthen our faith?
- Do you strive for worldly status? Is it really wrong to want to 'get ahead'?

REFLECTION

How do Mr Gailey's 'lovely intangibles' connect to the Christmas story, and our ongoing faith in Jesus? Think about the 'lovely intangibles' in your own life. Are they being squeezed out because of other, less important things? Is God asking you to take a risk for him? Perhaps he is asking you to take the risk of totally committing your life to him; getting to know him better; seeing more of your true identity and security in him as you believe more wholeheartedly; or stepping out for him in some other way?

PRAYER

Dear loving Father God
Thank you for the common sense you give us all in our daily lives. But Lord, please increase our faith so that when you ask us to do something, or believe something, that doesn't seem to fit in with our comfortable worldview, we are willing to take the risk of believing you and acting on it.
Amen.

WEEK FOUR
Nothing Impossible

Group icebreaker

Wrap a shoebox in Christmas wrapping paper, and hand it to the first member of the group. Ask them to talk about the greatest gift they ever received – or the greatest gift they would ever like to receive, however impossible it may seem. Then pass the box on to the next person, and so on.

On your own: Think about the greatest gift you ever received. Why was it so special? Who gave it to you? Alternatively, what would you like to receive? And who from?

To start

So far in these studies, we have looked at *Miracle on 34th Street,* along with the ongoing story of Jesus, God's Son, the second person of the Trinity, who came to earth to set us free from the terrible separation from God which humanity experiences as a result of sin. Now in Week Four of our explorations, Christmas is upon us. At this point, life can be chaotic, wrapping the last of the gifts, welcoming family and friends, and groaning as we receive last-minute cards from people we have forgotten to send them to. Time to take a breather, perhaps, and go outside into the still night air, looking at the stars, if it is a frosty night, and remembering the one who put them there.

As we prepare, during Advent, to celebrate the first arrival of the coming King, mysteriously born into the world by the Spirit of God, we can look forward, too, to the Second Advent, when Jesus will return. But whether Jesus returns or we must pass into the presence of God through death, the struggle really is to live for him *now*.

Why do I say struggle? Because living as a Christian requires faith in the unseen, and it isn't always easy in a world that doesn't believe. This can bring about quite serious problems. If we have come to know Jesus fairly recently, we may find some of our old habits incompatible with our new life in Christ. The closer we get to Jesus, the more we will discover what pleases him and what doesn't, by reading the Bible, the Word of God, and by the 'inner witness' of the Holy Spirit living in us, teaching us God's ways. Does something cause you to lose peace, or to feel uneasy? Check what you are doing/watching, or with whom you are spending time. Maybe it is the Lord, speaking to you about that situation.

Living full-out for Christ means not compromising with the world, so it follows that to maintain our walk with Jesus will cost us at some point. For instance, someone might ask us to take part in something we just *know* isn't God's will. If we carry on and do it, we will grieve God and very likely lose the sense of his presence. This can happen when we gossip, or get involved in other godless talk; or when we turn to a lifestyle we know is against God's will. If we used to join in with activities we now know are offensive to God and not his best plan for us, we may risk offending those who don't understand:

'You've changed. You're no fun anymore. Relax!'

'I feel like you're always judging me since you became a Christian.'

'Religion is fine, just don't take it so seriously!'

We may have to ask God what to do about relationships with friends, colleagues and acquaintances who tempt us into living in a way that isn't helpful.

Growing in personal faith and intimacy with anyone means spending time with them. The same is true for our relationship with God. To know him, we must spend time with him. As we do, we will find ourselves growing in confidence as we trust in him. We may hear his still, quiet voice in our very being and *know* what he requires us to do in a given situation. As we become familiar with his Word, we will understand more and more how to live to please him in thought, word and action. As we grow closer to him, living in obedience even in difficult situations, we will begin to experience the delight of God 'turning up' for us in unexpected and sometimes thrilling ways.

When we don't join in with some of the things the world enjoys and calls fun, people may think our belief is at best boring and at worst miserable. But that is far from true. When the disciples walked with Jesus they discovered a different life – a life full of surprises and excitement. It is worth reading the story of Lazarus in John 11, if you have time (perhaps after the relatives have gone to bed, and the remains of the turkey are all cleared away). The disappointment of a beloved brother lying dead in the grave when Jesus *could* have turned up and healed him turns into sheer amazement and wonder as a man is raised from the dead after four days in the tomb. What a miracle! A greater miracle than 'merely' healing a sick person.

As we read in the Bible of Jesus and his many miracles, signs pointing to who he was, we may wonder what has happened to the miraculous today. It is miraculous that God came to earth as a baby and grew up and died for our salvation. But healing the sick? Casting out demons, and seeing people changed because their attachment to the occult is broken? Do we see that today?

When we *don't*, part of the problem may be our Western civilized mind-set. In some respects we live in a faith-and-wonder-immunized society. If we see someone healed after prayer, people may explain it away: 'Ah, they'd get healed anyway.' We are used to cynicism. But while genuine 'healing miracles' need to be substantially verified, we shouldn't negate the work of a supernatural God.

A little while after I first became a Christian, I was suffering from oral thrush. No amount of visits to the doctor could cure it. At that time, I went along to a celebration meeting, and the visiting speaker suggested we all started praising Jesus out loud. At that point, this was something I had never done and, frankly, did not *want* to do. Anyway, I took a deep breath, focused totally on Jesus, and worshipped. As I did so I heard someone speaking in a different language – and I realized it was me. I had been baptized in the Holy Spirit and was speaking in tongues! Awestruck, I thought, 'Crikey! If God can enable me to speak in a language I haven't learned, as they did back in the days of the Acts of the Apostles, surely he can heal my oral thrush.' I was healed of that painful condition at that very moment and never had trouble with it again. That isn't to say I didn't go on to have other health issues at a later date; but that healing happened, and I knew, just *knew*, it was the grace of God.

Coming to Jesus, we need to have the faith of a child who believes their Father can do anything. The greater our faith, the greater miracles we will see. But we can't 'work faith' up. We need to get closer to Jesus and, trusting him, begin to rest in who he is, his free favour for us, and who we are in him. It's when we see him more clearly that we can begin to believe him for the impossible.

PAUSE FOR THOUGHT
Ask God to increase your faith this Christmas!

Watch 01.19.00 – 01.20:20; 01.21:53 – 01.22:22

This clip shows us the beginning of a change in

Mrs Walker, as she talks with her daughter about Kris Kringle. The way Kris *is* as a person is what makes Susan believe that he really is Santa. He is everything she expects Santa Claus to be.

Susan decides to write a letter to Kris to cheer him up. In it she writes that she believes everything he told her, and even that he will get her the present she asked for. As this is a beautiful (real) house, it would seem very unlikely. But in the letter she is really affirming that she believes in him, in who he is and what he has said, and that he will do as she has asked. That's faith.

And a turn in faith is also seen when Mrs Walker adds 'I believe in you, too' to the letter. This means more to Kris than anything else.

PAUSE FOR THOUGHT
Think about Susan's child-like faith. Remember when you first believed. Is your faith as 'fresh' as it was then? Has anything happened to dampen your expectation of what God might do in your life?

Think about

Is Jesus everything we might expect God to be? Let's think about that. If he accurately reveals the nature of the true and living God, then we see a God who loves us so much that he makes a way for us to have unbroken fellowship with him – even though

we are the ones who went astray in the first place.
The account of the prodigal or lost son in Luke
15:11-31 is a good picture story of this. Acceptance
and forgiveness followed by lavish generosity. That
kindness and perfect love is the God we worship.
As we look at the acceptance and loving-kindness
of Jesus in the Gospels, the compassion which
changes hearts and lives, we get an accurate view of
what God is like in the person of a man.

What is it about Jesus that really tugs at your
heart strings? Is it the way he weeps with the sisters
of Lazarus, joining with them in their grief? Or the
way he says 'Don't cry' to the widow who has lost
her son (Luke 7:11-17)? Is it the way he accepts
people without condemnation, such as the woman
at the well in John 4:1-26? This is our God. Do we
really, *really* believe in him?

PAUSE FOR THOUGHT

*Is the real God, as we see in Jesus, the God you
believe in?*

Watch 01.26:47 – 01.27:24

This short scene reveals a lot about the essence
of true faith. The fact that Mrs Walker asks Kris
Kringle to Christmas Eve dinner shows that in
reality her faith is not, at this point, very real. If she
has written 'I believe in you, too', indicating that
she believes that Kris is Santa Claus, why would she

expect him to be free on Christmas Eve, when Santa traditionally delivers his presents? Perhaps Doris Walker doesn't really believe in the miraculous …

PAUSE FOR THOUGHT

If Mrs Walker believes Kris truly is Santa, why do you think she doesn't believe in the 'supernatural' part of who he is?

Think about

Just as Doris Walker's words reveal that she only partly believes – and so therefore has not had the life-changing experience of actually finding out that Kris really *is* the real Santa Claus at this point – so our words (and actions) reveal what we truly believe. Often the Jesus we say we believe in stays safely in a manger, or on the cross, but isn't allowed to intrude in our day-to-day lives. Why is that? Is it because he seems far away? Is it because we think he isn't the same person today as he was when he walked and talked with people in the flesh? Do we think the miracles were for those days, and not for today? Why is that? Because we have the canon of Scripture and we don't need miracles anymore? Does the Word of God say that? Do we lack faith because we don't really believe his Word? Sometimes we pay Jesus lip service. We say we believe, but our actions deny it.

It is good, therefore, from time to time to really

examine what we believe about the child who was born in Bethlehem 2,000 years ago. Is our Jesus a 'safe' Jesus? Have we got him in a box, like a Christmas present, but we have never actually opened the package and found out what it means to truly have Jesus in our life?

There is a good picture of the Christian life in the form of a house. We might hear his gentle knock at our door, and open to him, welcoming him into the hallway. But that's as far as he gets. We don't want him in the kitchen, or the living room. If we do allow him access to other 'rooms' in our life, we certainly don't want him poking about in our dusty old cupboards. Who knows, he might make us chuck out something we are keen to hold on to.

We limit Jesus in our lives. He is a gentleman, and his Spirit will never force his way in. He *invites* us to follow him, and he *asks* if he may come in. Our part of the deal is to say 'yes' – or 'no'. It's our choice. We have as much, or as little, of God as we want.

Our God is a supernatural God. Surely the greatest miracle of all is that he came to earth as a man, to save us. If we believe that, do we really believe that he can do extraordinary, life-changing things in our own lives? Some of those things might be uncomfortable for us. Perhaps he wants us to deal with something we don't actually want to face, before he will move to bless us. Will we let him?

PAUSE FOR THOUGHT

In what areas of your life are you paying Jesus lip service? Do you believe he is able to work miracles, large and small, in your life and in the lives of those you love?

Watch 01.26:19 – 01.31:53 (1994 version)

In the older version, it is all the letters to Santa Claus that have been delivered to the post office over the years that are dumped in the courtroom that sway the outcome of the hearing. I think the newer version is a lot more powerful, and that is why I have chosen to use it here. Mr Bedford (the Gailey character) gets Susan to give the judge a dollar bill, bearing the words, 'In God we trust'. As there is no way to prove the existence of God, and yet the declaration of faith remains, so, the judge rules, it is a similar thing in regards to the existence of Santa Claus. You simply can't disprove him. So he makes the announcement, 'Santa Claus does exist and he exists in the person of Kris Kringle.'

PAUSE FOR THOUGHT

Do you agree that we cannot prove the existence of God? Why/why not?

Think about

Following on from that pause for thought – is it really impossible to prove the existence of the living God? When we look at the natural world, can we honestly say we don't see him? Psalm 19:1 says, 'The heavens declare the glory of God; the skies proclaim the work of his hands.' When we peruse the book of Job, chapters 38 to 41, we find ourselves, with Job in chapter 42, awestruck.

Many people who have faith in God can attest to remarkable 'coincidences'. I once prayed for a single thing – for six years. People told me that what I wanted was impossible, and I *did* want to stop praying for it because it seemed so unlikely when every single door was shut. Then, one day, I was walking my old black Labrador, Timber, and I said to God: 'Father, I've prayed for six years for this thing. I think I got it wrong. I am giving up. But I have to tell you, this has done *nothing* for my faith!' That was a Tuesday, and I felt pretty despondent. But by the Thursday, I had a casual conversation with somebody, and half an hour later received a phone call telling me that what I had prayed for, for six years, was about to happen. This helped my faith quite a bit, as I am sure you can imagine.

I have found, in my life, that by taking our eyes off the impossible situation, and fixing it on the one who can do the impossible – that's where faith starts. In the circumstances I mentioned above, I had lost faith in what I was praying for. But I still knew Jesus. Since that time, I have prayed earnestly for other things and not, as yet, received them. But I still know Jesus. We may not always get the answer to prayer we had hoped for, but as we look back at our faith journey, and believe God *can* do the miracle, we have to trust that for our good and his glory, he chooses not to … at least, at this time.

When things are tough, we can lose sight of God and who he is. Especially if the trial is ongoing, over a period of months and perhaps even years. But at the end of it all, when we look at the person of Jesus Christ, especially as we approach Christmas Eve – which always seems so special to me – I wonder if we can say: 'God does exist and he exists in the person of Jesus Christ.'

PAUSE FOR THOUGHT

Do you believe that God exists in the person of Jesus Christ?

Watch 01.27:25 – 01.29:30

When Susan realizes Kris Kringle hasn't got her the present she asked for, she immediately loses faith. Her mother tells her she should believe in him, but Susan didn't get what she wanted, and so believing doesn't make sense to her. Mrs Walker responds with the wonderful: 'Faith is believing in things when common sense tells you not to.' Obviously Doris Walker's trust issues have been challenged and changed. Having been let down by her previous husband, it seems here as though she is accepting that she can love again.

PAUSE FOR THOUGHT

Being so let down by her previous partner, Doris Walker has allowed bitterness to corrupt her life and, tragically, the life of her daughter. Here, we see the ice beginning to thaw. Do you have any 'rooms' in your life that you are reluctant to open up to God? What do you think may happen if you let him in?

Think about

When people let us down, we can often choose to shut the door, never trust them again, and never trust God, either. The root of bitterness can grow into a big tangled plant if we are not careful. There is an oak tree that grows just outside my garden. Currently it is being choked by ivy, which will have to be removed shortly or the tree will die. We can be like that tree when we allow resentment, unforgiveness, frustration, disillusionment and regret to choke the life out of us. It is then that our love for God may grow very cold. We can feel as if we are going through the motions in our faith, and that is all.

Anger and the following depression can be like dark, heavy blankets settling about our shoulders. In that state we can shut out the light of hope, of love.

We push people away because we've had enough of being hurt. We can't deal with it any more. Better to cut off and feel nothing.

Mrs Walker, in the film, has opened herself up to love with the amiable Mr Gailey. Having once been terribly let down, she seems willing to take a chance, a risk, in love, once again.

But people aren't infallible. Our ultimate trust should be in the one who will *never* let us down.

We may perceive, of course, that he has. We didn't get the answer we wanted. The boss didn't change his mind about our job. The doctor still gave us bad news. The desperately longed-for baby never arrived. The great career never happened. Our husband/wife still wanted a divorce. Our loved one suffered, or died. At those times we may ask, where was God?

My mother has dementia. When I eventually had to put her into a care home, I sat in the car and asked God – 'Why?' And I saw a picture of a white sheet of paper, all scrapped over with dark lines and ruined. But in the middle of the picture was a stick person – I knew it was me. And there was another stick person beside me – and that was Jesus. I felt him impress upon me: 'I'm in it with you.' Sometimes, we have to leave it at that. People leave us; sometimes they want to, and sometimes they don't. They disappoint us, and we disappoint them. We are only human. Only God will never leave us or forsake us (Hebrews 13:5). But he doesn't always give us what we want.

The thing is, we know that God is good. We know

God loves us. Therefore we have to trust him with his decisions as we commit them to him. Some answers we won't get this side of heaven. Faith means still believing, even when – yes, common sense says we should walk away.

PAUSE FOR THOUGHT

Have you felt let down by God? By other people? How did this affect your relationship with Jesus?

Watch 01.29:31 – 01.32:13

'I believe, I believe,' says Susan. 'It's silly, but I believe.'

This is really the apex of faith – when we still believe when all seems lost, when everything we hoped for seems to lie in dust and ashes; when the thing we hoped for, the outcome we had desired and asked for doesn't just seem unlikely, but utterly impossible.

And then, at Kris Kringle's direction, Mr Gailey's car arrives at the very house Susan has asked Kris for. She is still murmuring 'I believe' when she sees the house. Thrilled, Susan runs inside … her faith in Kris Kringle has been proved right: 'I kept believing and you were right … ' she tells her mother, 'Mr Kringle *is* Santa Claus!'

Is it all a coincidence? Maybe.

But then Mr Gailey and Mrs Walker see a cane

by the fireplace …. Could it be that the old man really is who he said he was? Although both Mr Gailey and Mrs Walker have attested to faith, they are still obviously shocked at the thought.

Another miracle is, of course, the change in Mrs Walker. From doubting Fred Gailey, she now has someone to believe in; there is a traditional, romantic happy ending to the film.

Miracles happen. People change. Circumstances change. Miracles prove the existence of God, too.

But perhaps we have to believe first.

PAUSE FOR THOUGHT

Mr Gailey has just legally proved Kris Kringle is Santa Claus. So why do you think he and Mrs Walker were shocked when they saw the cane?

Think about

I don't know about you, but when I get a prayer answered I am often quite surprised. I suppose that shows where my faith really is!

I wonder how the disciples really felt when Jesus, risen from the dead, appeared to them. The Bible tells us they thought he was a ghost (Luke 24:37-39) and Thomas didn't believe at all, till he was given some substantial proof (John 20:24-28). We saw earlier, in Matthew 16:21 (for example) that Jesus had told the disciples he would die and be raised to life on the third day. That they didn't really believe him was manifestly obvious. I love to think of the conversation after they had witnessed the risen Christ:

'Did you see that? He ate fish!'

'I can't believe this … I mean, it was really him. Wasn't it?'

I wonder if there were any among them who nonchalantly shrugged their shoulders and said, 'Yeah, I kind of knew it all along. So what's the big deal? He said he was going to rise and he did. Did you doubt him? Hey, pass some of that fish over here … '? I don't think so.

Interestingly, we read later that the body of believers were gathered together praying for an imprisoned Peter, and couldn't believe it when their prayer was answered – see Acts 12:12-16.

PAUSE FOR THOUGHT

Are you surprised when your prayers are answered? Why/why not?

Into Advent!

Read: Luke 1:26–38.

It seems strange to leave the character of Mary till last here, when we are reading through an Advent course. But we need to see the enormity of the faith that she exercised, and the huge miracle that occurred because of her willing obedience.

By trusting God in this, Mary, a virgin, would have to trust God to work out the details. In today's society, it is a fact of life that few people are virgins on their wedding day. But in Bible times, it was imperative that the woman was 'pure'. Mary was pledged to be married. To become pregnant would be to immediately have people point the finger at Joseph – or to Mary herself as being what we might quaintly term 'a loose woman'.

On finding out she was going to have a baby, her betrothed, Joseph, had every right to not wish to continue in the agreement whereby they would be married. Engagements in those days meant rather more than they do today. Joseph's option was to quietly 'divorce' her, which seems a kind act, as he could have chosen to publicly disgrace her.

But as we know from Matthew's account (Matthew 1:18-25), an angel persuaded him not to do that and he obeyed. Joseph too, therefore, shows faith.

What a miracle – that a child would be conceived in this way. What a miracle that this child would be conceived by the 'overshadowing' of God's Spirit. What a miracle that God would send his Son to save us, so we need not be separated from him for all eternity (John 3:16).

As for Mary's faith, as her relative, Elizabeth, said to her: 'Blessed is she who has believed that the Lord would fulfil his promises to her' (Luke 1:45).

Sometimes we pray for miracles of healing, or deliverance. But surely the greatest miracle of all is that God so loved me and you that he sent his Son so we need never be separated from him … ever. What an amazing rescue story.

It is also the ultimate love story. While *Miracle on 34th Street* has a thread of romance in it, so we too have a golden thread of love running throughout our lives, if we have opened the door to Jesus. God *so* loved us that he gave, at such great a cost. And then he promises never to leave us.

What a beautiful miracle. Jesus really is Someone to believe in.

PAUSE FOR THOUGHT

- *How many miracles can you count in the Christmas story?*
- *Think about your favourite carol. How true is it to the story of the Nativity that we find in the Bible?*
- *Has God fulfilled his promises to you? Or are you still waiting?*

ACTIVITY SUGGESTIONS

- Think about the ice breaker activity at the start of this week's session. What is the one thing you would really like God to do for you, or for someone close to you? What is the one 'gift' you would like to receive? It might be something specific – such as a gift of faith. Write an honest letter to God. It might be that you have to finish the letter: 'I believe. It's silly, but I believe.' Trust God.

- If you have felt let down by God and other people, you may need to consider the whole area of forgiveness. It is worth looking at Christian books on forgiveness, including *Father, Forgive* by Robin Oake (Authentic), which is an excellent true story about forgiveness; *Insight into Forgiveness* (CWR) is also a good resource. An internet search would also reveal other helpful books about the subject.

FOR DISCUSSION

- 'When you forgive someone for hurting you, you don't let them off the hook, you let yourself off the hook.' Do you believe this? Discuss.
- The story *Miracle on 34th Street* is a lovely Christmas tale, and actually rather innocent. It addresses far deeper issues than we might at first suppose. Have a general discussion about the thoughts that have come to you during this Advent study. What has helped you? What has challenged you? Has your faith in God, who he is, and what he has done and is going to do, been strengthened?

REFLECTION

It is often when we 'let go and let God' that we see God begin to work in our lives. Is there an area in your life where you have struggled to let go? Perhaps it is something you very much want, and you can't take your hands off the situation, leading to frustration and disillusionment. Why not ask Jesus to give you the strength to let go, and rest in him, trusting him for the outcome? It may be more effective to see this process as letting Jesus in to a 'room' in your life that you have previously closed off to him. Perhaps this Christmas, you can open that door, and let him in.

PRAYER

Dear loving heavenly Father
Thank you for the wonderful Christmas story. But help us remember that it is not just for December, but for the whole year round. Let us never forget the wonder that God, because of his great love for us, became flesh and came to live with us, and died for us, and was raised to life for us, in the second person of the Trinity, Jesus Christ. Strengthen our faith and help us grow closer to you in the coming days, and weeks, and months. And help us to always remember that nothing is impossible to you.
Amen.

Conclusion

And so we come to the end of our Advent studies in *Miracle on 34th Street*. We have to say goodbye, then, to Doris Walker and Mr Gailey, to little Susan and the genial Kris Kringle. But while we might cease to think about this touching family movie, we must never cease to think about Jesus.

At the start of this book, I mentioned that I had been to a 'carol service' where the songs were a mixture of awesome fact and fantasy fiction. We need to separate the two. Make-believe can be fun – I've written and published fiction! – but real life isn't a fantasy. Real life can be tough. We can go through periods when everything seems good, but there are also seasons of difficulty in everybody's life. In a sense it is easy to have faith when the sun is shining and all is well in our world. But it isn't so easy when the dark clouds come, and sometimes remain for a long time.

But whatever happens or doesn't happen in our individual lives, the fact is, God is God. God is who God is. We should always worship him for the fact that he has revealed his nature to us, his very character and being, and chosen to do so in grace and mercy. The God who exists in Trinity – Father, Son, and Holy Spirit – will remain a mystery to us, and we will always be asking questions. But that he exists, and 'exists in the person of Jesus Christ' is, I hope, something that has challenged and encouraged you during these studies.

Long after Nativity scenes have been packed away and Christmas trees are being recycled, presents forgotten, the turkey eaten, and the indigestion tablets swallowed, Jesus remains in all his love for us as individuals. And in this cold, secular society, which appears to care so much about 'getting ahead' and so little about the 'lovely intangibles', we need to be, more than ever, vessels to show the light and love of our Lord Jesus to a hurting world. How can we do this? By getting closer to him ourselves. We become more and more like the people we spend a lot of time with. So let's challenge each other to spend more time with Jesus, and find out what happens.

I hope that this year, you will find that 'faith is about believing when common sense tells you not to', and that you will grow ever closer to your Lord. Believe in miracles – or rather believe in the God of miracles. As you fix your eyes on him, you will see him at work more and more to change you, and your life. It is, in reality, about putting him first, and letting him take care of *all* your needs. Let's not mix Jesus up with the world, at Christmas or during the rest of the year. Let's throw off everything that would take our eyes off him, as far as we can, and believe wholeheartedly in the one who gave his life for us.

People need something to believe in, whoever they are. Misplaced faith results in disappointment. But with Jesus, we can say although we may not understand, we can trust. Ultimately, he never disappoints, because he is good, and therefore his plans for us are perfect. This is someone greater than you and I. Someone greater than us all, and everything that challenges us. Small, and in a manger; grown, and on a cross; dead, and yet alive. This really is Someone to believe in.

It is possible that you have been challenged during the reading of this small book to commit your life to Jesus for the first time. Maybe you have never really thought about a truly 'personal' faith before. If that's the case, then a simple prayer to invite Jesus into your life will mean the start of your very own life-long Advent journey. Make sure to share with a Christian friend about what you have done, if that's the case.

Peace and grace be with you this Advent season, and beyond.